Daniel MacPherson

Reminiscences of Old Quebec

Subterranean passages under the citadel: account of the old convent of the Congregation of Notre Dame, that does not now exist: prominent old Quebecers, &c., &c.

Daniel MacPherson

Reminiscences of Old Quebec

Subterranean passages under the citadel: account of the old convent of the Congregation of Notre Dame, that does not now exist: prominent old Quebecers, &c., &c.

ISBN/EAN: 9783337328320

Printed in Europe, USA, Canada, Australia, Japan

Cover: Foto ©ninafisch / pixelio.de

More available books at **www.hansebooks.com**

REMINISCENCES

OF

OLD QUEBEC.

SUBTERRANEAN PASSAGES UNDER THE CITADEL
—ACCOUNT OF THE OLD CONVENT OF THE
CONGREGATION OF NOTRE DAME.

THAT DOES NOT NOW EXIST.

PROMINENT OLD QUEBECERS,
&c., &c.

BY

MRS. DANIEL MACPHERSON.

MONTREAL:
PRINTED BY JOHN LOVELL & SON,
1890.

Entered according to Act of Parliament of Canada, in the year one thousand eight hundred and ninety, by MRS. DANIEL MACPHERSON, in the office of the Minister of Agriculture and Statistics at Ottawa.

DEDICATION.

TO

JAMES MACPHERSON LEMOINE, Esq.,

AUTHOR OF

QUEBEC PAST AND PRESENT, MAPLE LEAVES,
ETC.,

MY DEAR HUSBAND'S COUSIN AND TRIED FRIEND,

I DEDICATE THIS VOLUME AS A SLIGHT MARK OF ESTEEM.

CHARLOTTE HOLT GETHINGS MACPHERSON.

CONTENTS.

CHAPTER.		PAGE
I.	Reminiscences of Quebec Fifty Years Ago	9
II.	Reminiscences of Quebec—*Continued*	22
III.	Charlesbourg	23
IV.	Murray Bay	27
V.	St. Helen's Island, Montreal	31
VI.	Little River St. Charles	34
VII.	Jeune Lorette	42
VIII.	Lake St. Charles	44
IX.	St. Leon Springs	46
X.	Two Great Fires of Quebec	48
XI.	The Ruins of the Suspension Bridge over Montmorency Falls	52
XII.	The Ursuline Convent; Roberval, Lake St. John.	58
XIII.	The Old Convent of La Congregation de Notre Dame	65
XIV.	La Tire Parties	68
XV.	Two Stories Founded on Facts	70
XVI.	My Godmother's Story	77
XVII.	Mount Hermon Cemetery	84
XVIII.	Prominent Characters of Quebec	88
XIX.	Spencer Grange, Quebec's Special Author's Home	100
XX.	Montreal General Hospital	103
XXI.	Notes on Nursing	107

QUEBEC AND ITS VICINITY.

CHAPTER I.

On stepping into Ye Olde Curiositie Shoppe, 2116 St. Catherine street, I saw exposed for sale an old oil painting of Place d'Armes, Quebec, in 1828. The proprietor, knowing that I had lived in Quebec, asked me if I recognized it. Know it—why, every house is rich in personal recollections. First, the grand old English Cathedral, that does not seem a day older than when first I saw it. On the lower side, the house for years occupied by P. J. O. Chauveau, Esq., late sheriff of Montreal; then Dr. Marsden's late residence; then that of Daniel Macpherson, and adjoining that then occupied by Hon. P. Casgrain; and, next to that, old Payne's hotel. Ah! what memories cluster around that old building. I have enjoyed many delightful reunions at Hon. Mr. Chauveau's, but, pleasant as they were, they are eclipsed by the glorious times we had in old Payne's hotel, where Quebec's renowned dancing mistress, Miss Aspinall, held royal sway, a very exacting queen in her own domain, with an eccentric horror of peppermints. Here we had the assemblies, and well do I recall the handsome couple, Mr. and Mrs. Hart's first appearance after their marriage—she who is now Lady Shea.

In this building were also exhibited the famous Siamese twins, Chang and Eng. In Catherine Crowe's "Night Side of Nature," she says, "I never saw them myself;" and, for the benefit of those similarly circumstanced, I quote the following particulars from Dr. Passavant:—

"They were united by a membrane which extended from the breast-bone to the navel; but, in other respects, were not different from their countrymen in general. They were exceedingly alike, only that Eng was the more robust of the two. Their pulsations were not always coincident. They were active and agile and fond of bodily exercises. Their intellects were well developed, and their tones of voice and accent were precisely the same.

"As they never conversed together, they had nearly forgotten their native tongue. If one was addressed, they both answered—(that may be, but I am positive I saw them speak to two different persons separately)—and a gentleman who is in this city told me only last evening he had seen them do so also." I continue Dr. Passavant's narrative:—

"They played some games of skill, but never with each other, as that, they said, would be like the right hand playing with the left. They read the same book at the same time, and sang together in unison.

"In America they had a fever which ran precisely the same course. Their hunger, thirst, sleeping and waking, were always coincident, and their tastes and inclinations were identical.

"Their movements were so simultaneous that it was impossible to distinguish with which the impulse originated, they appeared to have but one will. The idea of being separated by an operation was repugnant to them; and they consider themselves happier in their duality than are the individuals that look on them with pity. This admirable sympathy, although necessarily in an inferior degree, is generally manifested, more or less, betwixt all persons twin-born." I (the writer) can vouch for this sympathy myself. I have twin sons, men now living, who were always ill together. I remember on one occasion calling in Dr. Sewell to see my twin babies, about two years of age. "If one was ill," said Dr. Sewell, "I would say it was this bad influenza, prevalent, with tendency to inflammation; as both are ill, it may be something infectious." "Oh! no," I said, "both are always ill together." The dear old gentleman laughed at me and said, "did you ever see such a woman, she wants her boys ill in pairs." The next morning proved I was right, both were ill with inflammation of the lungs from bad influenza.

To return to the Siamese, a lady resident of this city told me only yesterday that she saw the Siamese Twins in New York, and had heard they had married sisters. One had two children the other three. They died about ten years ago, I think one twenty-four hours before the other. What caused the death of the other, I don't know, perhaps the separation, cutting of the ligature. I wish the Medical Faculty would tell us more about it.

We cross the road to the then residence of the Hon. Judge Black, now occupied by his nephew, J. G. Clapham, notary, adjoining which, in the picture, is a building (not now in existence) formerly used for some military service, in rear of which was the ill-fated theatre, the burning of which caused more grief than any one calamity that ever occurred in Quebec. It is with feelings of mingled awe and gratitude I allude to this, for only by a providential interposition were my father's family and myself saved from being there that night. It was a lovely evening and we were going, when my dear father said: "It is too fine a night to spend closed up in a theatre; let us drive to the MacPherson's and go some rainy night." Thank God, we took that drive; shall I ever forget our return to the city? We were living almost ten minutes walk from Place d'Armes, and the sky was one glare of light. I begged to go and see the fire. We got just opposite to Dr. Marsden's house I have described, when with outstretched hands we saw the Rev. Mr. O'Rielly approach, a much loved priest of the parish church. "Back, for God's sake," were his words. Shall I ever forget the agony of look and utterance "not a step further;" I thought in my ministration I was used to the sight of suffering, but I have never seen anything like this. I had just spoken to and given a drink of water to your dear friend Jane Scott and her father, and yet had to leave them to burn, crushed down under a load of staircase and people. The theatre had caught fire from drapery, a rush was made for the door, the doors opened inward, and when the staircase fell those who were near were buried in a mass with no possible means of extrication. Had no panic prevailed all might have been rescued, as was proved by one—quite a young fellow, George Shaw, brother of the present portwarden of Montreal, who held down his sister by force till another way was opened, and they were saved. Amongst other acts of heroism was that of Miss Ray, daughter of Am. Con. Genl. Ray, who, at the theatre with her sister and her intended, insisted her sister should be saved first, and when her betrothed returned it was too late, all retreat was cut off, and the last seen of them was the flames encircling them as they perished in each other's arms. So deep a gloom was cast over the city that the theatre was never rebuilt, and the rear of the present post office stands on its site. Let us turn to a brighter picture, the remembrance is too painful for continuance; and as in life the sad and the gay perpetually jostle each other, so it is here, with only the platform intervening but not shown in the picture, is all that remains of the ancient Castle of St. Lewis, now the Normal School. It was formerly used as the Governor General's residence, and my earliest recollections of it are a ball given there by Lady Aylmer to the young children. I remember going there, but that is all I remember about it, as I was then of the mature age of five years; but I do remember some years after an aunt in a pink silk turban going to another ball at the same castle, and as the guests were to promenade in the Governor's garden attached, we children were to go and look at them over the fence, but, alas, we had hardly got there when it commenced to rain, and we had to retreat. How many Quebecers are alive now that attended that ball? Opposite to this is the garden where is the monument erected in honor of Wolfe and Montcalm. Facing the river, only a few paces off, is the house where, in my day, resided the Hon. George Primrose, uncle of the present Earl of Roseberry. An aged relative, then seventy-five years of age, who had been absent from Quebec for fifty years, twenty years ago took me to this place and pointed out the house where my grandfather first lived. He was a Capt. James G.——of the old 100th Regiment. She told me at the time it was almost the only house, except one else I think between the road facing the river and the present residence of Mrs. White (Sir Hugh Allan's daughter). We now climb the hill and face the Citadel, and what a host of recollections are evoked here. I perfectly remember my nursery in one of the now Hunt houses, and breaking in the back of my doll's head to give it medicine, also my delight at seeing the Archery Club, the ladies held then. I don't think I have ever seen any more graceful pastime. Col. Gore, father of the present Countess of Errol, resided in one of these houses opposite to the Citadel, of which so much has been written. I will only recall a personal experience that will surprise even some old Quebecers. In the year 18— my beautiful cousin Lizzie Henshaw, the loveliest woman to my fancy in character as in person I have ever met, accompanied her husband to Quebec, the late lamented Edward Fayrer, of the Ordnance Department, on a duty of inspection as to stores needed. As he was starting for the Citadel, he said to his wife and us ladies, "I think you may come with me, and I will show you what you will never have again the chance to see probably, the underground rooms and passages with fireproof quarters for women and children, in case of siege." Can I forget the astonishment of the soldiers, when an official at the Citadel took out a heavy bunch of keys, and accompanied by a few soldiers, as a favor eagerly sought for, allowed to accompany us, opened double iron doors, conducted us down long steps till we reached a long passage only lighted by the holes for muskets, then pitch dark passages and large rooms suggestive of crawling insects. I remember the fear I had of being left behind, and said one might have to cry aloud to be heard if forgotten. The answer was no sound could be heard, and a soldier so left gave himself up to die, when he remembered he might be thought of when missed at evening roll call; such was the case, and when he did not answer, it struck the parties he had been with it was possible he might be found where he was, and so saved from a living tomb. I wonder if the Princess Louise or any of the Governor's ladies ever went through them.

And now, my friends, I'll give you a treat, from Mr. James Macpherson Le Moine's pen, of a letter I found in the Montreal *Star* in answer to the inquiry of an old Quebecer, Mrs. Daniel Macpherson.

OLD QUEBEC.

THE PLACE D'ARMES IN THE YEAR 1822.

To the Editor of the " Star ":—

SIR,—In a recent issue, an "Old Quebecer," now a resident of Montreal, has appealed to me for information as to the occupants of houses round the Place d'Armes, at Quebec, in 1822, in order to fully realize the objects shown in a curious old picture, of that period, owned in Montreal.

It is not always easy after a lapse of close on seventy years to re-people a locality with all its former tenants, even with the help of that eminently respectable authority—the "oldest inhabitant." I should have failed had I not had recourse to an ancient directory of the city, published at Quebec in 1822, at the printing office, 3 Mountain street, of Messrs. Wilson & Cowan, by one Thomas Henry Gleason, a very rare book at present. Beginning then with Mr. Morgan's emporium fashionable tailoring, I find that this large edifice, No. 1 Ste. Anne street, of which the corner-stone had been laid with grand Masonic honors on the 15th August, 1805, by the Hon. Thos. Dunn, then administrator of the province, was kept in 1822 as an hotel by one George Wilson, and known as the Union Hotel. The construction of the Union Hotel seems to have been quite a social event among our festive grandfathers. Chief Justice Sewell and other dignitaries were present in regalia. The American prisoners of war, taken in 1812, at Detroit, were installed for a short period in this hostelry, prior to their removal to the Chateau de Bonne, at Beauport. For years, those attractive social gatherings, the assembly balls, took place in the Union Hotel, then known as Payne's Hotel. It had originally been built on the site occupied about 1800 by the surgery of Dr. Longmore, staff-surgeon to the Forces, the ancestor of our respected fellow-townsman, Major Elton-Prower. At No. 2 an eminent barrister, member of Parliament, and finally chief justice, Vallières de Saint Real, had his law study and residence in 1822. No. 3 was occupied, later on, by the well-remembered president of the Literary and Historical Society, Dr. John Charlton Fisher, LL.D. Here was entertained by him, in 1842, on his visit to Quebec, the great English novelist, Charles Dickens. The house subsequently belonged to the Hon. Louis Massue, L. C. The corner dwelling, No. 4, was occupied by a noted builder, Mr. Fortier, was leased for years for Government offices, and subsequently owned by a noted and regretted Quebec physician, Dr. William Marsden. On the corner opposite to Treasury Lane, facing the Anglican Cathedral, there resided in 1822 a Mr. Joseph Roy, an uncle, I think, of the late Hon. P. J. O. Chauveau, who held out there more than half a century, in a roomy, old-fashioned house. To the west of the Place d'Armes stood the English Cathedral, erected in 1804, and a few yards north the old Court House, built in 1814 and destroyed by fire in 1871. Facing the west end of the Court House stood, and still stands, the Kent House, Prince Edward's winter-quarters in 1791-3, whilst, immediately to the east, there stood in 1822 the Commissariat office, purchased by the Ordnance Department from the heirs Brebant, about 1815. There was a gap, in 1822, where the Union Savings Bank now stands, and across it to the east was the house and office of the late Hon. Louis Panet, senator and N. P. The corner dwelling and law office, now owned by James Dunbar, Q.C., was probably tenanted in 1822 by its late owner, Barthelot D'Artigny, Barrister and Member of Parliament. To the east, loomed out in 1822 the lofty wing of the old chateau, burnt on 23rd January, 1834, now tenanted by the Laval Normal school, then known as Chateau Haldimand, built by him in 1779. A high wall and a guard room adjoined, with the old building used for years, first as a riding school, and in 1846 as a theatre, whose destruction by fire, on the 12th June of that year, was attended with a great loss of life. The corner house, in 1822, was owned by James Black, the father of Judge Henry Black, now the property of John Greaves Clapham, N.P. Until 1863 the Place d'Armes was an open space on which the militia roll was called each year on the 29th June, St. Peter and St. Paul's day. Possibly the regulars, the 70th, may have drilled there in 1822, and the spot may have also been familiar to Paymaster Thomas Scott, the gifted brother of Sir Walter. In 1823 his remains rested in the St. Matthew Cemetery.

J. M LEMOINE.

QUEBEC, July, 1890.

CHAPTER II.

I saw in the paper a short time since that in the walls of Duquet's jewellery store, Fabrique street, had been found cannon balls or bullets. This is the very house old Mrs. L—— pointed out as the one in which she had been married. It was then occupied as officers' quarters. In fact, during fifty years absence, so little change had old Quebec seen that she pointed out the house, still standing, where her father had died, about four doors above Hope hill, left side going up. She could find her way everywhere till she came to the top of Abraham's hill—when she was completely lost. Why, this used to be all green fields. I used to walk out straight to the blue house and only another house, called the red house, for some miles. The red house is gone to give place to Tozer's residence. The blue house still existed a few years ago, and may still exist. The green fields are replaced by St. Roch's, the most thriving part of the city of Quebec.

CHAPTBR III.

CHARLESBOURG.

THE old gros habitant is a race very nearly extinct, at least in its distinctive features, for rich Canadians of that class have adopted the dress and ways of the present generation, whereas, in my day, however well-to-do a rich French-Canadian countryman was, he always wore the *étoffe du pays*, which was a pretty grey cloth, made amongst themselves, and superseded now by what is called Upper Canada tweed. I was at two weddings of the olden time, and as such are now extinct, I describe them for the benefit of those who can never have the opportunity of enjoying the fun of such long past days. If there are any of the people I speak of existant now, they will still be found, I think, only about the vicinity I now describe.

After passing the Pay bridge, St. Roch's, and turning to the left, we get on to the road leading to Lake St. Charles.

At the foot of Charlesbourg hill, a road turns to the right, which brings us to the small village of Ste. Angèle. A road so little noticed, that I am sure hundreds of Quebecers pass it every day without ever driving on it. The road lies low; all the houses are on an elevation, and side by side. About sixty years ago or more, the first house, a lovely residence, belonged to the family of the Hon. Jonathan Sewell, chief justice. In my young days it was unoccupied. Some legend of a man having hanged himself on a tree, in front of the house, caused the family to refuse to live there, and we children had the lovely grounds to ourselves; and many delightful walks and picnics we held there. This is now the residence of Mr. Alford, heir to Mr. Pozer (our almost sole Quebec millionaire then). He had bought up the ground on which St. Roch's now stands, and thus made a fortune.

Next to this was Mr. Giroux, gros habitant, then the Bourrets, then Villeneuves, then, Le Claires, and so on, for about a dozen farms, all thoroughly respectable, truly pious, with old French politeness, houses exquisitely clean. The women dressed on week days in flannel petticoats, and mantilettes of stuff spun by themselves. Well, old Bourret had only two daughters, and we had been in the habit of passing the summer there for many years, and we were of course asked to the wedding, for which grand preparations were in progress, and to celebrate which at least four houses were laid under contribution. The LeClaires were the violinists for all the country around, and their brilliant touch electrified all into motion. One house was used alone for dancing, and for three days and three nights the sound of quick moving feet was heard as they worked energetically in reel, jig and cotillion. One house was reserved for sleeping, where each, as they could get a chance of a bed, took a rest, and then again joined the dancers and gave place to others. One house only for cooking and eating, and the long tables, filling three sides of a room, were literally loaded down with provisions, replenished as fast as eaten. With genuine admiration, I viewed the array of ham, fowl, mutton, pork, beef, meat pies, with mountains of chrochinolles, or what they now call doughnuts or crullers.

Miss Bourret (now Madame Paquet) still lives, and these houses are still occupied by the younger branches of their families; but the gravestones in the churchyard of Charlesbourg church alone now record the abiding place of her parents. Near this church is Mr. Huot's well-known country inn for picnics, travellers, etc. Driving beyond this about ten miles on a lovely turnpike road, you come to Lake St. Charles, where the Verrets have a country hotel. The Verrets themselves are perfect specimens of the old rich habitant modernized, for the young ladies quite understand and follow the fashions as well as town ladies.

CHAPTER IV.

MURRAY BAY.

I think it is about fifty years ago that I went down on, I think, the first steamboat that ever went to Murray Bay. At that time it was only known to the friends of the seigneurs, Mr. Nairne and the Hon. John Malcolm Fraser. The steamer I think was called the "Pocohontas," and was styled by us clever young people as an old tub, because she had a good deal of motion and we were seasick. In fact, so great a storm arose, and we were so ill, that Mr. L. T. McP—— brother of the seigneur of Crane Island, offered the captain and all the passengers dinner and shelter if he would stop over for the night. I was so desperately ill I can remember little of it then, except the nice down beds and well spread meals for which the M—— ladies were so famous.

This is the island to which Mrs. Moody, authoress of "Roughing it in the Bush," etc. etc., alludes, in her work "Flora Lyndsay." "Thus, on the 29th of August, they passed Crane

Island, the beautiful domaine of Mr. Macpherson, on the north side of the river, and early on the morning of the 30th, the 'Annie' cast her anchor opposite Grosse Isle." This Mr. D. Macpherson, grandfather of James Macpherson Le Moine, and my dear late husband, gave the island to his son John, and his daughters devised it by will to a nephew, on condition that he took the name of Macpherson. He has not done so, but still has possession of the island notwithstanding. I suppose lawyers can arrange anything.

And now on to Murray Bay, where some of the happiest years of my life have been spent; but so full of sad as well as delightful reminiscences. I cannot linger over them, but will only say, that with the exception of one or two families besides ourselves, no one then went to Murray Bay but sportsmen and the friends and relatives of the seigneurs. Even ten years later our bread was sent from Quebec weekly, with vegetables, butter, meat, etc.; and at the post office, such a primitive institution, on receipt of the mail bag it was emptied on the floor, and every one helped themselves. Now it is crowded with hotels, fashionable visitors, and possesses a convalescent home,—a great boon to persons of limited or no means.

When we thought of going summer sea bathing, and we all of us had plenty of means then, our first visit was to the garret or old clothes cupboard, and everything shabby gathered together, and the purchase made of a good broad plaited and broad brimmed habitant hat, for which we paid about twenty-five cents (now sold for five), a large coarse red flannel nightgown for bathing dress, the very sight of which would cause any modern young lady to swoon away; but then we ladies went together, and for safety (instead of relying on beaux to protect us,—a horrid modern practice, I think) we joined hands and went in sometimes eight or ten together, and I am sure we enjoyed it more than the young people do now. Such drives in hay carts, almost jolted to death over rough roads. Archibald Campbell, Esq., and John Burrows, Esq., of the Prothonotary's Office, Quebec, and Henry Austin, Esq., I am sure still retain a pleasant recollection of these times. Previous to the trip I speak of in the "Pocohontas," Murray Bay was only reached by schooner. It was then renowned for its salmon and other fishing, as Crane Island was for its game. I don't know how it is now contemplated, when they tell me there is a railroad almost if not all the way to Murray Bay.

CHAPTER V.

ST. HELEN'S ISLAND, MONTREAL.

AT the period I write of was a military station only, occupied by soldiers and their officers and friends. I was sitting on the grass, with my dear cousin, Lizzie Fayrer, and her sister, Fanny Henshaw, also the army surgeon (I forget his name, but he was a splendid fellow), and a couple of young officers, when a loud detonation was heard. Some one turned laughingly to Fanny and said, "You are done for; that is the Grand Trunk blown up!" This was in allusion to the then secretary of the Grand Trunk, to whom she was engaged to be married. A circumstance I feel no delicacy in mentioning, as she has been his happy wife for the last thirty years, and is now living in England with her husband and a large family of children, all well and prosperous. We little thought how little fun there was about the matter. The surgeon was the first to perceive that there was something wrong, and said, "Oh! if I only had a boat, I would go and see;

they must want medical assistance." Having his case of instruments in his hand, he had been cleaning them. As he sat chatting with us, he said: "I'll risk taking a boat without permission. In a matter of life and death, surely red tapeism can be put aside. Will any of you ladies come?" We went. On nearing the shore, I caught sight of a figure under a sheet, and looked no more. Poor Lizzie insisted on going through the sheds and looking at every corpse, terrified that she might recognize her dearly loved brother George, who, though expected, had not come into Montreal that day, and I am happy to say is well and alive now, one of the few living links binding me to the happy past.

The noise we had heard was the explosion of the boiler of the Grand Trunk steamer, which caused many a warm heart to thrill with anguish.

I don't ever remember seeing such green grass as then on St. Helen's Island, and the butter was something wonderful, the grazing was so rich.

Now St. Helen's Island is covered with refreshment booths, wooden horses, and is crowded with excursionists every day in the summer. I doubt if there I could possibly recall the spot where I have had so much happiness. Mr. F—— lived there in the old barracks, and a little child of his lies buried, I think, in the churchyard there. All mementos left of one of the most genial homes I ever visited.

CHAPTER VI.

LITTLE RIVER ST. CHARLES.

AFTER leaving St. Rochs we pass out through what is the populous suburb of St. Sauveur 30 years ago. It was a pretty rural road sprinkled with cottages here and there. One still standing now belongs to the Robertsons, a little further out, three belonged to the late Major Temple, whose wife, a sister of Dr. Sewell's, was renowned, as so many of the Sewell family are, for her extreme amiability and gentle manners. I remember an anecdote she told me of herself. At the time she married, so little correct was the English idea of what Canada was, that even people well informed considered any one Canadian born very inferior to any one of English descent. Perhaps there are some who do so now? I only ask for information, not sarcastical, as Artemus Ward would say. Well, when the tenantry of Major Temple's brother heard that the major was going to marry in Canada, I fancy they pictured her as a sort of squaw, and their master, something of a farceur, rather encouraged the idea, at the same time insisting that, as his brother's wife and the daughter of the Hon. the chief justice of Quebec, she should be received with all the honors. Of course Mrs. Temple knew nothing of all this until after; and was thoroughly astonished to hear on every side: "Why, she is white." "Did they think I was a black?" she asked. "Something very near it, my dear, I think," was her husband's reply. She was a handsome woman in her middle age; if as fair in her youth as her daughter Mary was, they might well say she is white.

The next house then standing is that of Mr. Weir, where I lived myself until it was accidentally burnt down.

Mr. Weir was, I think, a civil engineer. I heard a few days since that his sons have realized large fortunes in the same line; and all met in Quebec a month ago. Such is the love we bear our dear old city, all those who can return to it when we can.

Now 30 years ago a queer old house greets our view, then occupied by Mr. Langlois, a retired country gentleman, living on his means in this pretty little house with his wife and large family. The original house had never been altered with the love our ancestors had for their homesteads, but a wing added on here and there as more room was required. If you do not meet Madame Langlois in one of the garden paths with large garden scissors in hand, you will catch sight of her bland hospitable face at the house door, you must come and partake of cake and wine *(de rigueur)* in those days, and then into the green house for a bunch of flowers. Very few of that large family survive, but I hear that Mrs. Buller (Dr.) and Mrs. Peterson, now living in Montreal, are her granddaughters.

We step here across the road to the residence of the late Judge Panet, father or grandfather of the present Minister of Militia. When first I knew it, it was occupied by a military surgeon, Dr. Reed and his family. The house interior arrangements were most picturesque and uncommon. You entered a hall whose ceiling was the vaulted roof. I have never seen anything like it elsewhere.

It had long been the desire of the Roman Catholic priesthood in Quebec to purchase a site for a cemetery. Application had been made repeatedly to purchase ground for that purpose to various people on the little river road, as it was called, but ineffectually; every person had lived half a century on their property, had plenty of means, and did not want a churchyard in the vicinity. Finally, on the death of Judge Panet, it was found, that persuaded of how much this burial ground was needed, he devised his property to the church for that purpose, and here adjoining the old house is the pretty St. Charles Cemetery.

The next property belonged then to the Hon. Louis Panet, senator, now owned and occupied by Hon. Jean Thomas Taschereau, ex-judge of the Superior Court, brother of the Cardinal, and his lady, sister of Sir Edouard Caron.

The Hon. Louis Panet's daughter, Madame Wilbrod Larue, then lived next door, and I have many delightful reminiscences of balls and fêtes of every kind, for then one danced as they took their tea—a matter of course. But it appears to me that ours were really the days of enjoyment. We understood the word fun I fear few young people understand now.

Near at hand now is the present residence of Judge Andrews, and opposite the pretty little cottage where not long since died his father and mother.

We now retrace our steps and come upon what is called Scott's bridge, on the right hand of which is the old King farm, and on the left a short distance up the Hunt farm, then Connolly's. And now, my children, I am going to take you to Poplar Grove, and introduce you to your dear father's early home and the dear grandmother you have never seen.

Entering the grounds by an old-fashioned wooden gate through a road of French poplars, you come upon a green circular grass plot on which we have danced many quadrilles. A gallery fronts a very large, low, neat-looking, unpretending building, and you enter a square, spacious passage, its furniture, a grandmother's clock, a comfortable sofa and same armchairs, on the left a pretty parlor and dining room in the rear. Straight on through the passage a door opens into a very large parlor, where a sweet-faced lady sits *netting* (not knitting). Netting is an almost forgotten style of female handwork. You ask what she is doing, and she answers: "I am not strong enough to go about much, so am amusing myself making a sett of curtains to be given to the one of the family to be married first. My dear husband was the first to be married and I got the curtains, unfortunately to be consumed in the fire that burnt the house." And now, children, with all love and reverence will I describe your dear grandmother, who from the day she extended her kindness to the motherless girl of nine years till the day of her death, almost a score of years after, was the object of my warmest affection and gratitude.

I see her before me now as she sits in that old-fashioned armchair, in her invariable dress of plain black silk, her snowy cap, collar and cuffs, with the dark hair with scarcely a silver thread, although she was seventy or more when she died, and that hair could reach to her knees. A handsome face, the expression that of perfect goodness and resignation, for she had known much grief. The death of two sons grown to manhood had clouded her declining years, and your father was the only male of the name of Macpherson belonging to the family. The advent here of my twin boys was consoling, but here again sorrow steps in.

In this dear old house died of scarlet fever my golden-haired little Kate, whose coffin rests on my mother's in old St. Matthew chapel cemetery, Quebec.

The side of this fine old room is half taken up by a bow window, spacious enough to contain a table and two chairs, and looking out upon a garden of tulips such as I have never seen elsewhere, gorgeous in all their purple crimson and gold, and, at the other end, a glass door leads into a porch with seats, and whose roof is hidden beneath morning glories and honeysuckles. A few steps takes you into the garden, where, under an immense walnut tree, we find seats and a table built around the trunk of the tree, so large that we sit down, perhaps, sixteen persons, every fine evening, to tea here, to enjoy the evening coolness and get rid of the flies. This tree was planted by your dear grandmother when a child, and under its shade she sat in her old age, for the property had been for generations in their family. But one night—a fierce winter one, in a raging storm—the family had to escape in their night-dresses and bare feet to a neighbor's house, the former property of Mrs. H——, an army surgeon's widow, who occasionally paid it a summer's visit, and were frequent visitors. Miss H—— still lives in Montreal; her sister, Lady M——, resides in Quebec; but Mr. P——, who housed them then, and continued a familiar visitor for years, has passed away.

Of your grandfather I need not speak. You remember him well, and the fine new residence built by him, but for which I would not give the old house. Now comes another Sewell—for no one could write the history of Quebec without speaking of them. Montague, son of the late chief justice, whose widow, daughter of old Colonel Wolfe, still lives at Portneuf with her two sons, her daughter married not long ago to Rev. Mr. ——, all these residences were bounded by the little River St. Charles, where the young people had boating to their heart's content.

CHAPTER VII.

JEUNE LORETTE.

In my early days there were really numbers of Indians, though the chief's baby was laid in a cradle and wore a lace cap. Now the relics of these times can there be seen, and not far off the house remains of old Madame Falardeau. A spacious, old-fashioned habitant house, very clean, with fine floors for dancing, and an immense supply of dinner equipage of the simplest style. We used to make up parties of thirty or forty, drive out and have real picnics, and Madame Falardeau made it a boast that she never forgot a face, and we never could catch her make a mistake. After an absence of many years a party went out, and one gentleman said, "Do you know me?" Madame Falardeau, after looking at him attentively, said, "You are Lord William Paulett, if he is in this country; but I heard he had gone to England." It was he; he had returned for a visit. And another lady went out with us one day, who had been absent thirty years. "Do you know me, Madame Falardeau?" "Yes; I am sure you are the little girl who always came out with your father, with a black boy in livery, a little black servant they brought to wait at table."

CHAPTER VIII.

LAKE ST. CHARLES.

I HAVE a picture of Lake St. Charles before me, painted for and presented to my father by the late Sheriff Sewell; and it contains a picture of my father's yacht and another boat,—a picture suggestive of such happy hours and sombre memories; and one fact rises up before me,—the singular fulfilment of a dream. I was at Lake St. Charles at the time and vouch for the truth, and also that four of the parties are still living. A party, consisting of a gentleman and two ladies, went out, and wishing to go boating, asked a young friend to take them out. He said it was too rough, as the wind was rising. They so persisted, and fearing they would go alone, he went to a young gentleman's house, a near neighbor, and asked him to come and help him to manage the boat. "Oh!" said Mrs. S——, "I don't want you to go, A—— it looks windy, and I am so anxious when you go on the water with a party." A—— positively refused to go, and when later it got quite windy, Mrs. S—— said, "I am so glad I persuaded you not to go." A—— answered, "You did not persuade me, mother; but I had one of my dreams last night. I thought I was in J. G——'s boat, with several persons, I did not see their faces, but the sail swung around and knocked over one person, who was lost overboard, so I took it as a warning." Before half an hour was passed, one of the party had been drowned in the manner described, despite the most gallant efforts of the gentleman who had tried to prevent their going, and had only yielded to the fear that they would go alone if he refused to accompany them.

CHAPTER IX.

ST. LEON SPRINGS.

It is fully fifty years ago since my father took me to Three Rivers *en route* for St. Leon Springs. We were most hospitably received by Mr. Lajoie, of Three Rivers (father of the present dry goods merchant of Three Rivers), and his good lady, and Mr. Faucher de St. Maurice, father of the present gentleman of the same name. Of the party were, I think, Mr. Gingras, whose son, brother-in-law of Mr. Dorion, recently deceased, was the first, I think, to establish the reputation of these waters. After a sumptuous repast at Mr. Lajoie's, we were driven to St. Leon Springs, and this is what I remember of it then, a steep sandy hill up which was walking a pale, thin young lady, whom my father pointed out to me as Miss G——; that lady has been in bed seven years, you see her walking now, whether the cure was permanent or not I have no means of ascertaining, but Mr. Campbell, late proprietor of St. Leon Springs, told me only two weeks since that he remembered Miss G—— perfectly. Mr. Campbell further told me since that his father had noticed the cattle drinking at this spring, and finding it had a peculiar taste, had it analysed, and gave to the public this boon for the afflicted and health-preserving drink for the sick. We had tea that day at the Springs on a deal table without table-cloth, seated on wooden benches, while carpenters were putting the roof on a large building we sat in. I presume this was the first hotel, rather a contrast to that of the present day, which is yearly crowded with an increased number of fashionable visitors from all parts of the Dominion, in search of health or amusement. This hotel has been very lately enlarged and fitted up with every modern convenience. Parties leaving Montreal by the Canadian Pacific Railroad, and getting off at Louiseville, will find vehicles waiting to take them to St. Leon Springs.

CHAPTER X.

TWO GREAT FIRES OF QUEBEC.

The great fire of —— commenced near the site of the present Frères' school, on Gallow's hill, as it was formerly suggestively called. It was supposed to have originated from hot ashes carelessly left in a back porch. We who knew the family living there scouted the idea, as they did; they were too methodical and good housekeepers to permit any carelessness. Only ten years ago, one of the daughters, now living, told me that a miscreant on his death-bed had confessed he had set fire to Mr. T——'s house, out of revenge for some fancied injury, and had led a life of torture, fearing discovery and grief at the widespread desolation he had created. But good results have followed, like the fire of St. Roch's; good substantial buildings have replaced old wooden structures. Have you ever heard the old-fashioned tocsin, "ding, dong, ding!" a fearful summons that seems to sound the knell of doom. We were in the playground, in our dear old Ursuline convent, when its first knell reached our ears. As usual, the good ladies sent out to ascertain the locality of the fire, and the report continued to come in—"ten, twenty, thirty, forty houses gone!" At last the Superioress appeared: "Young ladies, you hear how whole streets are going. We do not know where this will end. Take your choice now at once. I permit you to go home now, to be with your relatives. Later you may be unable to find them. So, if you desire to stay, you can do so, but will not be permitted to leave until to-morrow, unless sent for.

This fire was finally stopped through the heroic devotion of my dear husband's old friend, Archibald Campbell, Esq., advocate, of the Prothonotary's office. He was standing near General Hope when he heard him say, "If I could only get them to hear the order to blow up that house, we might stop the fire and save it from extending to the banks." "You would like to have that house blown up?" asked Mr. C——. "Yes," was the general's reply. "But no one could reach with the order in time." "I will," was young Archie's reply, and with the unreasoning disregard of self and courage he displayed on many other occasions, he leaped the rampart near the Hotel Dieu, flew down the cliff, and almost miraculously escaped to give directions and save further destruction. General Hope loaded him with praise. I wonder if any of those banks whose property was saved from destruction ever gave any substantial token of gratitude.

The Lewis suburb fire occurred a month earlier. It is a fact, but only came to our knowledge in a funny fashion. My dear old father was very particular about the get up of his linen, and had a special laundress. One morning he told the servant boy to go for his washing. On his returning without it, Mr. G——, whose old acquaintances will fully appreciate this, as he was known to be slightly quick-tempered, asked the reason, the boy answered, "Please, sir, I could not find Mrs. ——'s house." "Why not?" "She was burnt out." "Well, did you find out where she moved to?" "No, sir." "The next neighbors could have told you." "Please, sir, there are no neighbors." "Well, some one in the street." "There are no streets." "What does the fellow mean? Have you gone crazy?" "No, sir; please, all the streets are burnt up for ever so far." And such was indeed the case. We were living in a thickly walled brick house, opposite the present Morrin college (then the jail), now occupied by —— Chouinard, Esq. Ah! the many memories that cluster around that house. There my mother died! There I first heard the word "mesmerism!" My father said to Dr. Morrin, in my presence, "What is this stuff I hear about some power called 'mesmerism' possessed by some woman in the jail, I don't believe in it, do you?" "No," said Dr. M——, "I don't want to; but I have to against my own belief—as many must say, even in the present day."

CHAPTER XI.

THE RUINS OF THE SUSPENSION BRIGE OVER MONTMORENCY FALLS, QUEBEC.

About 30 years ago or more, the members of the Quebec road trust had decided on building a suspension bridge over the falls, to be used instead of one similar to that near Bureau's hotel, Montmorency.

It was completed to the delight of the trustees, but the habitants would not use it. They were unaccustomed to such a style of thing and considered it unsafe, and despite all reasoning would break off the bars nailed up to prevent passage over the other, and cross over.

To give them confidence, a party was organised by the trustees, and a lunch prepared for a party consisting of perhaps thirty persons of the most prominent families in Quebec, who all drove over, had a delightful time, and exultingly pointed to the fact of its safety in contrast to the fears of the rural population. The next day a woman and her son in a light cart crossed over, and the supports, strained by the weight of vehicles of the previous day and frost I think, gave way, and horse, cart, woman and boy were plunged in the seething waters. Had the catastrophe only occurred the day before, a dozen families instead of one would have been plunged into mourning. It was useless to dream of rebuilding it, it would never have been used by the people, and the stone supports can be seen to-day.

CHAPTER XII.

THE URSULINE CONVENT, QUEBEC.

I LEAVE to my learned friend, James Macpherson LeMoine, Esq. (brother of the recently deceased chaplain of this Institution), all historical details and mention of it.

I pretend only to personal reminiscences, and as every one in life has his use, I humbly creep in with my experience to fill the gap. I ought to know something of the dear old Ursulines, for from the age of nine years till a few months before my marriage, nine years after, I spent every day there, except summer holidays, from eight in the morning till five in the afternoon, taking dinner and lunch there, and so happy was I that I quite remember running into school, not away from it. The way was this, at eight precisely the heavy iron gates were opened by the Lady Superioress and another nun, and we filed in two and two between them; then once closed, no more to be opened till our exit, for the Ursulines is one of the strictest order in Canada. I was passionately fond of my school, my lessons and teachers, in fact, it was my home, for I was motherless, and the kindest of fathers cannot supply the mother's place, particularly when absent during the day on business. So terribly distressed at finding myself shut out, and too late, I was going away down-hearted, when I saw that the yard door was open, and old Louis, one of the factotums of the establishment, was sawing wood there. I remembered that passage led to the refectory windows, which were generally open at that hour. I made a dash past old Louis, jumped on the window with the celerity of lightning, doffed my bonnet, and quietly walked to class. Old Louis reported, but all was as usual when the Superioress came in to ascertain, and though I was not found out, I don't think even the good sisters would think it an unpardonable offence to run into school, though they might to run out.

This great establishment was then *par excellence* the educational seminary for ladies in Quebec, and even now when so many schools and new convents have been established, it still holds its own, for all the head nuns are ladies of liberal education, and their pupils come from north, south, east and west.

To an outsider the grim iron bars and the strict rules seem very distasteful, but if they only knew the happy placid life the inmates lead. Many of them are women of great talent. As I am writing of the past, I must refer to dear Mère de l'Incarnation, a South American lady, who seemed to me a walking encyclopedia, so various was her knowledge. Convent tradition says that a gentleman having inherited some property from Cuba, the lawyers were in a sad case, as no one understood Spanish sufficiently to decipher the deeds, when some one thought of this old lady, and the lawyers were then permitted to meet her in the parlor (the iron gratings intersecting however), while she translated the deeds. Another remarkable lady was the deceased Mère St. Henri, so beloved that she was constantly elected superioress; she was a relative of the seigneur of Murray Bay. I could go on for ever if I wanted to be discussive on the subject of these ladies. I will confine myself to the mention of only two more—one, Miss Georgiana Van Felson, now superioress, daughter of the late Judge Van Felson, an old schoolfellow, one of our companions on our first visit to Murray Bay. And last but not least, I must speak of my dear teacher and friend, Mère Ste. Croix, as smart when I saw her a few months ago as when I first knew her, some forty years since. She was a sister of that famous Abbé Holmes, whose work, "Conférance de Notre Dame," obtained a world-wide reputation. His eloquence was so great, that it was impossible to get through the crowd when he was to preach. My friends, no matter of what creed, if you can obtain a copy of Conférances de Notre Dame, they are published in English—though copies are very rare—you will enjoy a treat.

The first chaplain I remember there was the Venerable Father Maguire, who nearly choked himself, or was nearly choked, by bending too close over some chemical preparations at one of our examinations, for the young ladies even then in an advanced institution like the Ursulines of Quebec studied chemistry, botany, etc. Happily he recovered breath, but I have often since thought with horror how near we were to a tragedy. His successor was the Rev. Mr. LeMoine, one of those excellent men who live but for others. When curé of Beauport, his housekeeper used to complain that she dare not leave a spare blanket or second great coat in sight, for Mr. LeMoine would certainly give it away, saying, "why should I have a second article I do not need, when some one wants it?" I saw him a few weeks before his decease, his benevolent countenance all smiles as he said, "I am getting weak but do not suffer, and oh, every one is so good to me." H , so self-sacrificing for others, magnified everything done for himself. Once a nun of the Ursuline Convent takes the final vows after some years probation it is for life, and many of my readers will say this restraint is terrible, though voluntary. So far from it, by special permission of the Bishop, several of these ladies have left their convent to found institutions elsewhere, but invariably ask to be sent back to their Mother House. One of these, the Very Rev. Mère Ste. Croix, I mentioned, having gone to Texas (I think), returned a few years ago, and within ten years at most others returned from founding a convent of their order at

ROBERVAL, LAKE ST. JOHN;

and *à propos* of Roberval, let me say that

though I visited it under the most unfavorable auspices and in the bitter cold of an exceptionally severe winter, I was delighted with it; here the wild, wild country life with all the comforts of civilization. You leave Quebec on the train about 8 a.m., I think, and arrive the same evening. Just at the station are comfortable boarding houses. Even if the Grand Hotel is not open you have your daily post, your telegrams, even in the depth of winter. A few pleasant associates, good medical men, and a primitive existence most delightful to the town worn, and I cannot forbear mentioning with deepest gratitude the name of Mr. B. A. Scott, manager of large mills here. During the fearful epidemic of *la grippe*, that even found out this secluded part of the world, one of my sons was so ill with inflammation of the lungs from it that his life was despaired of. "There is no hope," said the doctors. "While there is life there is hope," answered Mr. Scott, and he recalled the doctors and stayed all night with my boy till pronounced out of danger. As he has done to mine, may others repay to him the debt in overflowing measure. His father had just the same kind nature, for I remember once in coming over from Crane Island (we were frequent visitors at the Misses Macpherson's hospitable home), a terrible storm arose. In a frail skiff we were almost lost. I was terribly ill and could not bear the wine and stuff offered me on landing, and he a stranger sent up a couple of bottles of bitter ale. I was able to retain a portion of that, and never forgot this instance of spontaneous kindness.

Roberval is destined, I am sure, to a grand future. Sensible people who want a change of air and scene get so thoroughly tired of the routine of fashionable life existent even at the well-worn sea-side places, that here, while enjoying all the comforts of civilization, you are really without its pale, and the air for many is much more beneficial than that of salt water. In fact, to many of those who are troubled with throat or chest affections the sea-side is decidedly inimical. Here you have the bracing, pure mountain air, which brings healing with every draft. Landing unexpectedly last winter I came suddenly to Mr. Thomas, and Madame Tremblay, though a stranger, with great courtesy, gave me up her own bedroom to make me comfortable. She is a nice musician. Her little daughter has a complexion of milk and roses, as also Mr. Tremblay's brother's wife, inherited from old country blood.

This very Mr. Tremblay, now living, told me he came here twelve years ago a dying man. His physician in California told him he had no hope, and, unwilling to leave a young wife in a strange city (they had come from St. Ann's, near Montreal), he made his last arrangements and came home to die, but instead inhaled new strength and health in the life-giving atmosphere of Lake St. John, and is living there now. I now leave it to Mr. Miller to describe with an abler pen than mine this beautiful region. The extract is from his "Doom of the Mamelons with a description of Lake St. John and Saguenay region":—

"And last, but not least, be it remembered by my readers, that from Quebec roll the trains of the Quebec and Lake St. John Railway, which for two hundred miles will take you through the least inhabited stretch of country crossed by steel rails on the continent; a country without houses or mills, or huts or cabins or wigwams, a stretch of real woodland, where on either side of the track stands a forest unmarked by axe, rivers on which are no boats, lakes numberless where no camp fire was ever lighted, and scarce an Indian's canoe has been, and where the beaver dams, on which the beavers were working but yesterday, are within forty feet of your window as you whirl past. Through this tangle of rivers, lakes, forests, swamps, hills, mountains, you are whirled onward until suddenly the train breaks, like a chased buck, out of the thicket, into an opening, and lo, the wide, bright waters of Lake St. John lie spread out in broad expanse before you. Verily it is worth a day's ride to see the loneliest lake in the loneliest woods in the wide world, is it not? And that, too, seen from the window of a Palace Car! It's enough to take an old trailsman's breath away to think of such a conjunction!

" The climate of the Lake St. John region, as I found it to be last summer, was a surprise to me. As it is two hundred miles directly north of Quebec, I naturally expected that it would be much colder. Instead of this being the case, I found the reverse to be true. Frost was much slower in coming than it was sixty leagues farther south. The water retained its summer warmth for nearly a full month beyond the date I had set for it to freeze. It was comfortable bathing at Lake St. John up to October 10, at which time the air was warm and genial. The prevalent winds were from the south-west, and they seemed to have blown from southern atmospheres, for even on stormy days they did not chill one. The cold east winds which blow straight up the St. Lawrence channel from Labrador, and which make one feel so uncomfortable at Quebec, and even at Montreal, seem not to get north of the Laurentian mountain line, for during all the autumn there was but one northeast storm, and that was not a cold one. I never lived in a more equable and genial autumnal climate than I found to be the normal one in this inland region, and for purposes of pleasure and health I can cordially commend camp life on these northern lakes until snow drives one out.

"Of wild fowl there is an abundance. Along the tributaries of the lake ducks and geese of many varieties nest and raise their young. The sportsman can find good sport both on the lake and on all the lakes around and in the rivers and streams flowing into it. In point of accessibility this region is now most convenient to all sportsmen and tourists from the States.

"The Lake St. John Railroad now runs to the very shore of the lake, and before reaching it, it passes scores of lesser lakes full of fish and beautiful to the eye. No angler need go to Lake St. John to command as good angling as a disciple of the rod ever found. But if he is ambitious to try his skill and test his tackle on a wan-na-nish, that peer of the salmon, he must visit the great lake, for in no other body of water in the woods can he find this noble fish. The angler leaving Boston Monday morning will reach Lake St. John Tuesday afternoon, and cover the entire distance in a Pullman car. This makes an excursion even of a week's duration practicable to any angler from New England. I know of no other opportunity for prime sport to be found on the continent equal to this. The opening up of this wonderful country to the public by the construction of this railroad is a positive boon to sportsman and tourist alike. It makes a high order of pleasure and healthy recreation possible and convenient to thousands that could not otherwise enjoy it.

"It should be remembered in this connection that all this country is yet in a wilderness condition, and, therefore, most charming to those who love seclusion, and from education in camp life and woodcraft know how to guide and take care of themselves and those dependent on them for needed protection and comfort. But there are a few hotels and but few settlements or clearings, and "guiding" is not a practice or a habit of life with the Indians and half-breeds resident there. These needed facilities of safety and happiness will, undoubtedly, be speedily evolved from the rude conditions now existing in answer to public demand, but at present they do not exist to any such extent as to be adequate for any great multitude of visitors. I don't doubt that the natives, both red and white, will speedily develope into excellent guides, for many of them are experts in canoe service and at trailing and their trapping life has made them familiar with the country, within certain fixed limits."

CHAPTER XIII.

THE OLD CONVENT OF LA CONGRE-GATION DE NOTRE DAME

I WAS born in the old Quebec Bank, Quebec. I don't remember the circumstance myself; but I do remember being drawn in a basket-carriage by old Germain, the messenger of the bank, to the Convent, situated on the site occupied by the Gibb stores and those of Messrs. McCall & McShene.

The Convent was so near the water that, as an inmate of the Convent of the order told me to-day, the sailors, not being very backward, used to land their boats so close that the sails used to flap on the Convent windows.

The present Convent of the Sisters of the Congrégation de Notre Dame has been forty-seven years on its present site opposite St. Roch's church, on St. Joseph street. So it is quite fifty-six years since I learnt my letters in the old building on St. Peter street, and since my father used to call at the Convent for me and take me out boating on the St. Lawrence river, then the ordinary place of boating for lovers of the water; but how I hated it, it made me so ill, and poor father would always persist in saying it was the fat soup I got for dinner at the Convent. The effect of the soup must have lasted many years, for I was always ill on the water, until about twenty years ago. I went down in the autumn to Charlottetown, P.E.I., and the weather being very rough I bribed the stewardess to put a mattress on the floor of the cabin and bring me my meals there. I never got up till we arrived at Charlottetown, and though both stewardesses were ill, and all the other ladies, I was not so at all. I attributed it to lying down from the first moment —a hint for others suffering with *mal de mer*. I hope it may prove equally successful.

The Convent at Ville Marie, Montreal, is the *maison mère*, or head convent of the Congrégation de Notre Dame.

My next recollection of the Quebec Bank was when Mr. Noah Freer was manager. I particularly recall a parcel of biscuits he shared with me at lunch time; and many years after, about the last time I saw the old gentleman, I asked him if he still kept his biscuits there, and he showed them to me in their accustomed nook.

CHAPTER XIV.

LA TIRE PARTIES.

I THINK I hear my old country and American readers say: "What is La Tire?" Now, don't be horrified, your own fair hands work up flour in buns and pastries, and you eat the latter made by you know not whom, when purchased. Well, la tire is a candy made by boiling molasses to a certain consistency—only the experienced can say when exactly cooked enough. The general plan is to put a spoonful now and then into cold water, and when it snaps it is done. A lump is then taken up in flour powdered fingers and pulled until white. An amateur will do this without scarcely touching it, and so neatly she could do it with a velvet dress on and not leave a speck. It is undoubtedly the healthiest and the very nicest candy I think ever made. A kind of imitation of it is sold in the confectioners, but inferior, I think, to the genuine article. Well, fifty years ago St. Catherine's day was always looked forward to as a great time for the young folks, and we always hoped by that day to have some sleighing and also la tire parties. Fancy twenty or thirty even grown people making la tire, each one vying with the other as to whose was the whitest. Such fun, such threats from some one that unless some request for a dance or something were promised you would be surrounded by a string of la tire and be stuck all over. These parties were gradually dropped for more fashionable assemblies, but some French Canadian families still make it for their young people every now and then.

CHAPTER XV.

TWO STORIES FOUNDED ON FACTS, WRITTEN FOR MY DEAR LITTLE FRIEND BELL HOLT, DAUGHTER OF STANLEY HOLT, ESQ., TREASURY DEPARTMENT, QUEBEC.

IN a second hand hotel in the lower town of Quebec lay dying a poor lady, widow of an officer in the army, whose demise had only occurred a year before. Like many military men, this gentleman, whom we will call Mr. Smith (for I will not give his real name), had been most anxious to purchase a farm and work it, and because he had thought little of the discomforts he enjoyed out sporting, imagining life in the country was to be a perfect paradise. It is comparatively easy to gather the crop when ripe, but what of the planting and hand-work to be gone through before arriving at that end. However, he was not destined to face these trials, for he caught a cold in carelessly exposing himself when on a shooting excursion and also one of investigation, looking out for a suitable purchase in the then wilds of Valcartier. He died of rapid decline after a short illness, and left his wife and children to do as best they could with the few hundred pounds left. Mrs. S., like most officers' wives, knew little of household management, accustomed to have their rations regularly sent in, wood and light provided, and an orderly always at their service. Even a military man himself, once he leaves the army, generally finds he is helpless in these matters, and quite dependent on the honesty of those about him. Hence poor Mrs. S. was in a sad plight, for they had not been many years in this country, and their principal friends had been the members of the regiment to which Mr. S. had belonged; they had gradually slipped out of sight and memory of their few remaining acquaintances in Quebec. All alone, with only a grasping, coarse-minded boarding house mistress standing beside her bed, she passed away, begging of the woman to go to a clergyman and ask him to take what money was left, and seeing who her relatives were from papers in a box she gave her, try and send her children to them. It was most unfortunate that this poor lady should not have seen to these important matters herself while able; but she had been so completely prostrated by her husband's sudden death that she had deferred the matter until too late, and she found herself unexpectedly face to face with the grim conqueror, and so these poor children had to suffer alone for the procrastinating sin of their parents, for though the woman promised she did not perform. On the contrary, she indeed got the little girl into an orphan asylum, but the boys being older, one was sent to Valcartier to help on a farm, and the other, though still very young, was apprenticed to a boot maker.

The clergyman who came to the funeral service did enquire if there were no friends or means, but the woman said only enough was left for funeral expenses, and hardly enough to pay what was due for the board of the family during the father's and mother's illness. This of course was untrue, but she as soon as possible disposed of the children in the aforesaid manner, hid away or destroyed the papers and took possesion of money, trinkets and everything the poor lady had left.

A year passed when another officer's widow (Mrs. S.) asked her daughter if she could not get her a little servant to thread her needle and sit beside her to perform any little offices needed, for she felt herself growing very infirm. Accordingly a visit was made to the orphan asylum, and struck by the pleasant, refined face of this little Miss Smith she was selected. Some time after Mrs. S. was going to receive some company, and extra silver dishes and pretty china articles were brought out for use. The little girl helped in doing so, but displayed no astonishment at the sight of what Mrs. S. thought must be a wonderful sight to the child. At length Mrs. S., curious at the child's display of indifference, said: "You may look at this silver basket, child. I don't think you have ever seen anything so pretty before." "Oh, yes, I have," promptly answered the little one. "Mamma had things like you." Fancying this was only the outcome of childish pride, Mrs. S. said sharply: "My child, you are not speaking the truth, these things cost a great deal of money.' "But;" persisted the little one, "mamma did have things like that, and she had a gold watch and a piano—my mother was a lady."

Mrs. S. growing interested gradually drew from Miss Smith her whole history. "Child," she said, "what was your father's name?" "He was Captain Smith." Growing quite excited, the old lady called her daughter. "My dear, you have often heard your father speak of his old comrade Captain S. Well, if what this child states is true, this must be his poor little neglected child." A responsible party at once went with the little girl to the Lower Town Hotel, and the landlady's confusion at the sight of the child was so great that it was evident she feared detection, and by threats of sending her to jail, she was at last induced to confess the whole thing, and return the mother's effects and part of the ill-gotten money. Can you fancy the meeting between these long-parted little children, for old acquaintances of their father's came forward to claim them, and they were tended by loving hands until their relatives in England could be communicated with, and as then there were neither steamships nor telegraphs, it took many months. Once more enjoying the comforts of life together the time flew quickly, till at last came kind letters from grandmother and uncles, urgently asking that they be sent home to them at once, and there we leave them. The mother's long deferred prayer for her little ones was at last heard, and the Father of the fatherless had had them in His keeping as He has us all; only when bowed down with grief and trials we cannot realize that the discipline is needed. Perhaps the very privations these poor children had suffered might prove the means of greater happiness later by teaching them to appreciate our daily comforts taken as a matter of course, and for which we are so little grateful.

This true story was told me by an old blind Scotch lady, Miss O., who, having outlived all her relatives, was supported by her friends and the Presbyterian church of Quebec. Speaking of her changed position, though residing a few doors from us in a pretty farm house at Little River, she said that when showing kindness to the little girl, how little her mother thought her own daughter would be dependent on strangers in later life, for she had only an officer's daughter's pension. And now, young ladies, shall I tell you to what she attributed her blindness,—an almost criminal neglect of her eyes. Exceedingly fond of fancy-work, she occupied herself with it unceasingly, and as her sight grew weaker, she used stronger light. One evening she said she was just finishing a bit of work, and twilight coming on, she strained her eyes by going to the window, exerting herself to finish her work, when all became dark and was dark forever.

CHAPTER XVI.

MY GODMOTHER'S STORY, TOLD BY HER TO ME SOME TWENTY-FIVE YEARS AGO.

SHE came on a visit to Quebec after an absence of many long years; and seeing me in great trouble then, though up to that time my life had been an exceptionally prosperous and happy one, said, "Don't loose heart. To all there comes a period in life when individuals seem singled out for misfortune, death enters and claims not one, but successive victims, till it seems as if our troubles were greater than we can bear. Yet, at last, there is a rift in the cloud, the darkness rolls away, and the sun of prosperity shines again, doubly appreciated after the period of gloom.

I remember well this lady's home, her daughter was my companion, but a few years old, and it was with keen admiration, and I fear a little pang of envy, I contemplated her numerous and expensive toys sent for her form New York—quite a journey then, fifty years ago; but Mrs. W. was very rich, and had an elegantly furnished house opposite the wall of the old Jesuit barracks in St. Ann street, in rear of the old Ursuline convent. And now permit me to digress a little while I tell you a funny incident that occurred to some young ladies in the same convent. The Ursuline convent forms a square, the front facing St. Lewis street, the back bounded their own property on St. Anne street, and their garden extending from opposite the English Cathedral to the rear of the Sewell property on St. Anne street. Well, some old gentleman lived in one of these Sewell houses, and in his yard was an apple tree, whose branches loaded with fruit hung over the garden wall, too tempting for modern Eves to resist. We were given plenty of apples for dessert at our convent dinners, but these forbidden fruit were supposed to be sweeter, and some of the young ladies found means of getting at and appropriating the fruit. This coming to the ears of the good sisters, punishment swift and severe for the delinquents was to be meted out. These good ladies considered the offence enormous. What, convent girls so well brought up to be guilty of such dishonest, unlady-like conduct! So it was decided the girls should go and ask the old gentleman's pardon, acknowledging the offence, and word was sent to Mr. A. (we will call him), who said he would be glad to see them. An hour was appointed for the reception, as he did think they should arrange the matter personally. They were sent under the charge of some head servant of the establishment (for the Ursulines never leave their convent, except to found other convents by order of the Bishop), and very shamefully and rather nervously entered a parlor which contained a table loaded with sweets and confections. An old gentleman with a very benevolent and smiling face greeted them thus: "Young ladies, I am very glad that the anger of the good sisters has procured me the pleasure of this visit and of you a holiday. You will not refuse to partake of this slight lunch I have had prepared for you, and take home to your young companions this basket of apples and sweets. And now, one all I make you a free gift of all the fruit of my trees. I cannot use it myself, and shall be glad if you young ladies will have it." Such was the punishment meted out and the ineffectual attempt of the convent authorities to impress on them the difference between mine and thine; and now I must return to my dear godmother. Her father, a wealthy American, had brought her, a motherless only child and settled in Quebec. So delicately was she brought up, that she had even a little black boy in livery to carry her books to school. Yet with every wish gratified, so noble was her nature, she did not become selfish, for she told me herself that the greatest comfort she had had in her adversity was that she had so frequently sent letters with money anonomously to other friends who needed it, but to whom the giving of it personally would have given pain. At the time of her marriage she told me she had no idea of how to sew, had never indeed even hemmed a handkerchief.

She continued living with her father for years after her marriage, and a nurse who had lived with them, and served me after, said she heard old Mr. F. say one day exultingly of his darling daughter's fate and happiness: " Thank God, my child can never want." No doubt a thoughtless but a terrible speech to make— almost enough to invoke misfortune. Many a king and queen has wanted for bread, and any eflecting person must know there can be no possibility of security from trouble, much less from money loss. Even when all precautions are taken, can any one say that their wealth is secure? Money invested in buildings may be lost by large fires, causing the insolvency of insurance companies; banks may fail; and business speculations may turn out ill. And such was the case here. Mr. F. lost money, and the disaster so preyed upon him, that he fell ill of brain fever, and the first news his wife got was that he was dying at Lake George, U. S. She hurried on there, but traveling was so slow that she only arrived in time to receive his dying breath. The news so prostrated her aged father, that he became paralysed and could not help her, and she who had been bred up in the lap of luxury found herself almost penniless in a strange part of the country with a father who required a masculine attendant, he had become so helpless, two sons and a little daughter. Happily for her then, as at all times she was a sincere christian, and she committed her cause to Him who doeth all things well. Thinking over the future she said to a friend, " I have had a good education. I can at any rate educate my children, why not educate others also ? " So the idea was acted on. She opened a school at Glen's Falls. She told me that when she knelt down for the evening prayer, the first time she was there she thought her heart would break as she caught sight of the carpetless floor, the bare wooden tables and benches. Her eldest son, seeing her emotion, came up, and putting his arm around her said : " Mother, dear, do not fret, good times will come again," but to her good times seemed impossible. Yet some years after when my father and myself on a trip to Saratoga tried to see her, we were told that some wild lands, belonging to her father, considered worth nothing, had become valuable, and that she had gone to Chicago. Later, on the occasion of her visit to us in Quebec, she said to me, " My dear child, I do not say this out of ostentation, but to show you how the wheel of fortune turns, and bright times come again, as my son said. I was present at his wedding in Chicago, where there were three hundred invited guests, for he had married the daughter of a very rich man and was doing well himself. As I gazed at the brilliant party crowding dining-room, hall, parlor, and conservatories, I did indeed realize that good times had come again."

CHAPTER XVII.

MOUNT HERMON CEMETERY.

THE sun was shining and the birds were sending forth their joyous peals, as James Macpherson LeMoine most kindly drove me to my husband's grave. I had been too ill to go there at the time of his funeral, and even now, my son said, " You should not go, mother; you cannot stand it." How thankful I am I did go. The peacefulness of Mount Hermon seems to have passed into my heart. I have visited the grand cemetery of Mount Auburn. I have often seen Mount Royal and Cote de Neiges. But the quiet peacefulness of Mount Hermon excelled them all.

I only saw a couple of mourners at the graves, and my darling's resting place pleased me much. A good sized nicely kept plot, not grand with bright colored flowers, but nicely kept green mounds indicating each resting place; a plain granite to his father's memory, beside whom and his mother and his little child he sleeps. "Adieu, my darling. I go forth with my bitter grief much assuaged to leave you in such a quiet resting place, afar from the jar of a city where crowds do not congregate with their hampers, as is done elsewhere." I do not think our dear departed wish us to sorrow uselessly, but there certainly appears to me a want of reverence to the dead when the cemeteries are turned into picnic grounds.

"The long, long dreary day is past and gone,
And still I am weeping, my lone watch keeping."

TO MY DEAR HUSBAND, WHO DIED 15TH AUGUST, 1889.

As I sit in the gloaming and ponder,
And grieve for the dear one no more,
Like a wind-toss'd bark on the ocean,
I long for a sight of the shore
Where storms are unknown and safe shelter
Awaits those who faithfully strive
His heavenly footsteps to follow,
Our *Saviour*, who, dead and alive,
A loving example has set us,
And beckons us onward to share
The heavenly mansion he promised
And went on before to prepare.

On the banks of Death's lonely river,
Extending I see your dear hand;
Tho' long be the years intervening,
You'll wait for me there on the strand,
And be the first spirit to greet me,
On the shores of that heavenly land.
So I'll shoulder my cross with submission,
And patiently wait for my call,
Content that in death's silent slumber,
That you should be spared grief and all
That a life's separation implies.
Whose lives have been twined so together,
Full forty-five years, aye and more,
The wrench is so great, it seems almost
The cord is so strained it must break;
But now, husband darling, I leave you,
In peace in Mount Hermon to sleep,
While I, better fitted by nature
To struggle with grief and to weep,
Await here that blessed to-morrow
Will take me to meet you again.
For love that is true love will ever
Spare the loved one all pain and all grief,
And gladly itself bear the burden
To give that loved other relief.
Then sleep on in peace, my dear husband,
Beside father, mother and child,
While I in submission abide,
Till on death's call I hasten
Once more to your loved side.
And have I not also our children
Whose love and whose duty combine
To replace all I've lost in you, darling.

Yet, in death, as in life, you are mine.
And the words that you said on your death bed
Are ever before me, my dear,
"You cannot stay very long after,
The end of your life is so near."

CHAPTER XVIII.

PROMINENT CHARACTERS QUEBEC.

HIS LORDSHIP THE LATE BISHOP MOUNTAIN.

I cannot revisit the old English Cathedral in Quebec without seeing in the glass of memory the venerable figure of Bishop Mountain, in his lawn sleeves, seated in his place of dignity near the altar railing.

So many are living who can recall his kindly face, I do not need to give him an elaborate notice. He was universally respected and beloved, and with wise and cautious policy held his own at a difficult crisis in the Anglican church's history in Quebec. His deacon or curate (I am not sure of the title), also much liked, was decidedly low church, as were most of his congregation; but this was the time of the Puseyite movement, and his son, the Rev. Armeyn, just returned from Oxford, decidedly high church in his views, but the dear old bishop, by his moderation and personal force of character, abated the storm, and there was no split in the Cathedral congregation. I will not dilate on his good qualities, but I will only relate one circumstance that will, I think, serve to illustrate his character. The seigneur of Crane Island, John Macpherson, died there, and his body was taken to the south shore to be buried. Remark, at that time there were neither telephones, railroads nor telegraphs. A man in a sleigh breasting the heavy country roads, crossing the river from Levis in a canoe, amidst shoals of ice, brought the intelligence, and also the request for a clergyman to perform the funeral service. What was to be done? Any clergyman consenting would have to face the dangerous crossing and then drive about 25 miles in intense cold and storm. Mr. L. T. Macpherson saw but one plan of action, to lay the matter before the Bishop, this being the only way he could think of to accomplish his duty to his dead brother and his nieces. An appeal was made to the Bishop, and what do you suppose was his answer, thoroughly characteristic of the man, " It will be such a disagreeable journey that I should not like to request any of the clergy to go, they might construe it into a command; but I will go myself. I am an old missionary, you know, and used to hardships." And he did go. Noble old gentleman that he was. This narrative alone embalms his memory.

THE REV. FATHER McMAHON.

One of the most celebrated priests of the Irish parish church of Quebec, a prototype of the Rev. Father Dowd, here beloved by Protestants as by Catholics. Well, the Rev. Mr. McMahon was one of those men without fear and without regard, who could always hold his own, and on one occasion, when there was some little sign of a rupture between Protestants and Roman Catholics, he quietly turned round and asked his own congregation if they would remember that St. Patrick's church was mostly built with Protestant money. They acknowledged the fact, and harmony was restored. On another occasion he heard giggling in the gallery, and turning his eyes upon the delinquents—two or three members of the most respectable families of his congregation, he said : " Young ladies, if this disturbance continues I shall have to ask the beadle to call you out by name and request you to leave the church." Need I say the lesson was most effectual, and was it not justly given? Even apart from irreverence, can there be worse manners than for any two or three persons to disturb a whole congregation, either in church or other assembly? Perhaps some of our modern young people will think of this when they talk loud in theatres and public places when the performance does not suit them, regardless of the rights of others.

JEFFREY HALE, ESQ.

The name of the venerated Jeffrey Hale is a household word in Quebec.

" If by your works ye shall know them," he will be well judged.

A practical christian embodies all we have to say.

A man of aristocratic lineage and ample means, he showed his blue blood by his truly refined, unostentatious life. His thin, spare figure, his benevolent face, and that of his sister, a refined lady of the old school, will not readily be forgotten by Quebecers. His Sunday School Jeffrey Hale's hospital and St. Matthew's chapel bear witness to his liberal disposition of money for charitable purposes. St. Matthew's chapel was the first place of worship in Quebec where the pews were free. It was intended for poor people, but is now the most fashionable church in the city. Adjoining is the old English burying-ground peopled by our fathers and grandfathers, and containing the last remains of many an English officer. A dying sister said she would rather have Mr. Hale talk and read to her than any clergyman.

COLONEL ANTROBUS.

Col. Antrobus, the then one military aide-de-camp, and just the right man in the right place, handsome, dignified, overflowing with *bonhomie*, a favorite with all, fell a victim to cholera, I think, and died after a few days illness, deeply regretted.

THE HON. R. E. CARON,

afterwards Sir R. E. Caron, mayor, judge, lieut.-governor, who for good looks and graciousness contested the palm with our dear old Dr. Sewell. We use the term here as a mark of affection for Dr. Sewell never grew old, always suave and cheerful, and attended his patients till a short time before his death.

So great a favorite was the Hon. R. E. Caron, that quite a number of years was he mayor of Quebec. He was constantly re-elected, his fellow-citizens recognizing the fact of his peculiar eligibility for the office. Generous in entertaining, with ample means, his handsome house in St. Louis street (where some members of his family still reside) was the house of gracious hospitality, and when raised to the position of lieut.-governor, it was generally conceded a wiser choice could not have been made. He retained his popularity until his death.

His successor was, I think, Hon. Mr. LeTellier, who, being a widower, and his daughters young, prevailed on Lady Stuart to receive his guests on reception nights. This lady, member of one of the oldest and most respected French families of the olden time, was well fitted by habit and position for the office. The DeGaspé family belong to the annals of Quebec from Mons. DeGaspé, senior, author of that very rare and interesting old book, "Les Anciens Canadiens." Like the Philips family, they were all very handsome. I only remember a few of them,

Mad. DeBeaujeu, Mad. Alleyn, Madame Power, the Abbé DeGaspé, Madame Fraser and Madame Hudon. Is it really the case that the past generation were handsomer than their predecessors, or is there truth in what an English officer, Capt. Warberton, wrote on Stadacona, Quebec, that whereas he had never seen in Canada such real beauty as he occasionally met in England, still he had never met so many pretty girls as in Quebec. But I remember the gentlemen as well as the ladies, and a sight to be admired was that of Mr. Philips with his son and daughters, as they walked to church, each and every one beautiful. Several of them have passed away. One I know lives in Montreal, Mad. B——, wife of the Q.C. of that name. She was very handsome, and one of Miss Aspinall's most proficient scholars.

I wonder whether the young people now are ever taught the graceful scarf dance, or stately minuet. It is about twenty years since I went into society, so can only write of the past not the present.

Leaving the Caron's residence, we see on the right hand side a comfortable stone house where lived the High Constable Downs. I think his daughter, Mrs. B———, still lives there. The old gentleman, I remember, was very stout and rather tenacious of the dignity of his office, and was a little quick-tempered, quite enough to make him the subject of a practical joke which created a great sensation in my time. Some graceless young fellow (lawyer, they say) stole a number of summonses signed by the High Constable, and ready for filling up, commanding the receiver under any amount of penalties not to fail to appear on the petty jury. These were sent to people of the highest position in the city exempt from any such service, and the very sending of which implied gross ignorance on the part of the sender. Fancy then the scene that appeared in Mr. Down's office, when a gentleman, a judge I think, who knew it was a mistake, showing the document to Mr. ———, said, "Is there not a little error here?" "A little error! No, sir, there is a great error here, and the dolt who sent out that paper shall certainly be dismissed for not knowing his business better." But in comes another and still another dignity of the law with the same work, until it dawned upon these gentlemen that they had been all hoaxed. They laughed, but not so Mr. D———. This was touching the majesty of the law and his office, and he swore dire vengeance on the delinquent for stealing his papers, when he should discover the offender; but despite all efforts, the secret was well kept, only some who knew our incorrigible *farceur* suspected.

PADDY McGUIRE, AN HONEST HORSE DEALER.

"Well, Miss Charlotte," I think I hear him say, "sure I'm glad to meet ye. I've been looking for ye this week past. I've just the loveliest little pony, canters beautiful—just the thing you want for your own pretty self. I'm keepin' it for ye. You'll just spake to Pa about it, won't you?"

"I could have sold it over and over again, but you see I wanted you to have it." "But Mr. McGrath, you know, we have a nice horse already, and my father only keeps one." "A nice horse, faith, and who knows better than myself. Sure didn't I sell it to the old gentleman; but because you have a good one, can't ye have a better?" I don't think I got the pony; but, wherever procured, I had plenty of riding, and with my darling husband used to think nothing of a ride out past the Suède, and home to Little River.

HOT-ROLLS.

Is there any one in Quebec that remembers Hot-Rolls. A *soubriquet* for a poor unfortunate gentleman whom drink and disaster had brought so low, that his only means of living was bringing around hot rolls for some baker. I have reason to remember him, for, on one occasion, when all alone in the English Cathedral, he walked in, drew out a big long knife, and sat down at the entrance end of the pew, depositing the knife on the shelf before him. I was when young very nervous. I was terrified beyond expression, and sat in agony till the gentleman came around for the collection in my father's pew, when he induced him to leave, and once more I breathed freely.

MRS. HEUSTON.

I do not think that there could be a better illustration of the thoughtlessness regarding lunatics some fifty years ago, than that illustrated in the case of Mrs. Heuston. It was said she had seen better days. I was too young to remember much about her, but I do remember a wild creature dressed in old finery—her head decked with flowers, low necked and short sleeves, then evening dress, wearing white satin slippers, and so dressed coming for contributions to Mrs. Hammond's school in the depth of winter. How could our ancesters have permitted such a thing for a day? The answer is perhaps due to the fact that lunatic asylums then were abodes of horror; that freedom to this poor creature, though she would not wear warm clothing, was doubly precious, as I have it from my dear father's authority, that once on a jury he had visited the primitive asylum, and there had seen bad patients: one, a sister of a medical man in high position then, was given her food through a trough like pigs. And aneut prominent personages, I may mention Dr. Douglas. I hardly think he can be living now. He, in conjunction with others, opened an asylum on the Beauport road. I remember my father saying to him: " Well, Doctor I have just been talking to one of your patients who is as sane as you are, perhaps more so, as you wrongly judge him a lunatic." "Well," said the Doctor, "go and ask him what countryman he is." My father did so, and in a state of great excitement (he had touched his peculiar monomania), he answered:

"I am father of the Moon and cousin to the Sun, and all bow down to me." Dr. Douglas was a man of intellectual taste, and had a lovely residence then on Beauport road replete with articles of virtu. I do not know who occupies it now.

CHAPTER XIX.

SPENCER GRANGE, QUEBEC'S SPECIAL AUTHOR'S HOME.

RARE OBJECTS STILL AT SPENCER GRANGE.

The first I remember of Spencer wood was as a visitor at the then residence of Mr. Atkinson, a rich merchant of artistic taste, and who in his travels had collected many curiosities. The next time I went there was at a reception of the governor's ladies, for Mr. Atkinson had ceded it to the government as a vice-regal residence, and removed to a smaller dwelling. Spencer Grange, I remember, was a thoroughly respectable, comfortable house, nicely furnished, but though presided over by a niece, yet emphatically the residence of an old bachelor. Last week I visited Spencer Grange, and I am happy to say the feminine element predominates, and he (Mr. A.) only plays second best. What can a man do against three of the higher sex? It is true he has his library as overflowing with books as his own brain with knowledge. We leave him there guarded by an animal Miss Jeannette calls a beauty. As I am far from the indignant flash of her dark eyes, I will express my opinion and say if her pet is good-looking, I nevertheless mistrust him. "Oh! I can assure you," says Miss J., "he is so kind and such a good breed, and is only cross to trespassers." And have I not reason to be uneasy? He knew I was a trespasser when he came and looked me over, and discerned I was going to devour his master's substance. After a preliminary sniff, which expressed, "I'll take you on trial," he left me to wend my way into the pleasant parlor, I have known so many long years under such different circumstances. But I must not moralize here; the cup of grief is full, and if I permitted myself to be a moment off guard it would overflow. So I will put all painful thoughts aside, and ask you to look out on the pretty lawn skirted with forest trees, then follow me into the dining room, adjoining which is a passage adorned with marble busts, leading to the grapery—a sight worth driving miles to see when the grapes are in bloom. I do not think I noticed one article which would tempt you to ask the price, unless it be a curious mosaic marble, brought, I think, from Italy by Mrs. LeMoine's uncle, Henry Atkinson. When I was young it was considered that the mingling of colors in a lady's dress should be so blended you could not think of detail but of the harmonious whole, and such is the effect of the interior of the Grange. Harmony, comfort, elegance without pretension, specially noticeable is the bedroom *par excellence*, the ladies' department.

The grounds about Spencer Grange are not extensive, but the house is so situated that wherever you look you see a miniature wood, you could fancy yourself a dozen miles from the city instead of three. Mr. LeMoine has added a new front, which gives extra room and takes off from the plainness of the old building. The architect deserves credit for the skill he has employed in its construction. Such a cosy little sewing room, flanked by the most comfortable of bedrooms, where good taste prevails in the coloring and ornaments. One thing specially noticed was the heads of rare wild animals, and in every corner trophies of the chase. A pretty aviary also adjoins the dining room. I hope it may be many years ere death or sorrow invade its presence.

CHAPTER XX.

THE MONTREAL GENERAL HOSPITAL.

Permitted by the kindness of the officials to sit for many hours a day for several weeks beside the bed of a young Englishman, who had no relatives in this country, and who required constant watching, I had an opportunity, given to few outsiders, of seeing thoroughly the working of this institution, and, though the old prejudice against hospitals has died away, and I had come to recognise the nursing as far superior to that possible in a private house, I had no conception of the perfection to which the arrangements have been brought in this establishment. In fact, had I to choose between leaving a sick friend at a well regulated hospital (even as a non-paying patient) or at a fine hotel, I should choose the former, knowing they would be better cared for than in any outside institution wanting hospital appliances. When all is so well conducted, it is hard to discriminate. From the dignified matron, Miss Livingston, to the under-nurses and assistants, all work thoroughly and cheerfully; but, as it was in Ward 11, where I had my part of observation, I must be excused if I mention specially the refined head nurse, Miss Chapman, and her assistants, Miss Hobson and Miss Priam. The two former are English ladies, and the latter a clergyman's daughter from Upper Canada. The extreme delicacy with which they discharge often disagreeable and painful duties is beyond all praise, and Miss Chapman, being an educated lady with considerable medical knowledge, I would rather take my report of my friends condition from her than from that of the attending physician, because while he sees the patients at certain hours, she sees them at all times and can note things he cannot. "Am I right, Dr. McReeves?" I see the doctor's beaming face and courteous bow as he says. "You are right, madame." And now permit me to say, in my humble opinion, that he Montreal General Hospital still wants two things to make it perfect. As this article is written without any one's knowledge, I alone am responsible for the suggestions that may possibly bear good fruit, but cannot do any harm, so I will venture to remark, I think the two things most needed in connection with this institution are a convalescent home attached to or near to the city, conducted exactly as the hospital itself, with intelligent nurses to take care of patients well enough to leave their beds, but yet requiring weeks of care, a change from the sick ward when sleep is not liable to be disturbed by sicker patients, cheerful surroundings and pleasant companionship, instead of the sight of others' suffering, must surely be an aid to recovery; and two separate wards for ladies and gentlemen of refinement but small means who cannot afford a private room.

I fully recognise the fact that the non-paying patient has all the care and luxuries ordered for his case as much as the one who pays $60 per month; but how much more comfortable a lady with moderate income, or clerk on small salary, would feel if he could get to the ward set apart for such cases, and pay a moderate sum as he would in a boarding-house, and in the end I think it would pay, for so many would pay some pounds per month who give nothing now. Think of this all ye in high places, let the grand corporation of the Canadian Pacific and Grand Trunk with its hundreds of employees, some of whom are always in this institution, ponder seriously on these facts, and may God lead them to think to purpose and bring into action with good result. Are we not all interested in this matter? What may not a day bring forth? Who is to say but to-morrow we ourselves, our sons, daughters or brethren, may not find ourselves at the mercy of this or some similar health-restoring home.

If the Canadian Pacific Railway and Grand Trunk Railway were to donate a sum they could easily spare for a few wards I have spoken of, they could be kept up by contributions and money received for boarding patients of a better class, who in the time of illness would be specially sensitive to surroundings.

CHAPTFR XXI.

NOTES ON NURSING.

THIS part of my book must necessarily be egotistical, if I am to help others by my advice and experience. I can only do so by saying what I did myself and how I came to do it.

Well, in the year ———, a young son of mine was sitting on the Esplanade, Quebec, watching some exhibition, when he found the party seated beside him was a young girl covered with small-pox. He left quickly, but the harm was done. I forget how many days after he took ill. The late lamented Dr. LaFleur, of Levis, attended him, and from him I learnt the treatment, which enabled me, alone, without nurse or physician, to treat another son. Both were very bad cases, and neither bear the slightest mark of ever having had the disease.

I wished to go to the General Hospital in Quebec with my boy. "What is your object?" Dr. LaFleur inquired. "To prevent giving it to others," I answered. "Well," he said, "as you would have to get a carriage, cross in the steamer, and drive some distance, you would probably do your son great harm and risk infection to dozens of people before you get there." So I remained where I was. We occupied a very large double house; one side-parlor and bedroom was tightly closed off from the rest. All food was carried to me by an old man, hired to sit on a grass-plot and bring what was required—taking it from the servants' hands and depositing it on the gallery. Every article of furniture was taken and, with carpet, put in the hangard, and there kept three months. I only retained a bed, and I had a small stove, in which I burnt all remains of food, and the plates were thoroughly soaked in disinfectants before being returned to the cook. All linen and bits of cotton used as pocket handkerchiefs were burnt, and the sheets thrown into tubs of cold water, with disinfectants, and the old man, with a stick, shaking them around several times, before changing the water, and put them out on the grass, in the hot sun, to dry; thus I could change the bed every day or two, and yet not risk infection to others by having them washed. Dr. LaFleur only came into the house for about a week, he looked at his patient through an open window. I attended him alone for six weeks, and then two tents were erected, in one of which he and I sat and talked to other members of the family in another tent. This was the one solitary case in South Quebec. Thank God no one took it from us. And now for my second case and the treatment:

I must premise I pretend to no medical knowledge. I never gave a pulse or temperament to a doctor, for my days were the days of Dickens' Sarey Gamp, and to give a drink, or rather not give a drink, of cold water to a fever-stricken and thirst-consuming patient was the utmost we aimed at in nursing; so that in acting the part of sole physician, I was driven by stern necessity by no desire of my own.

When first the small-pox epidemic appeared in Montreal, there was a regular panic, there was not room in the Civic Hospital, and the doctors feared to attend small-pox cases on account of the fears of their other patients. This was the position of affairs when I went one morning to my dressmaker, and asked her to make some small repairs to a pair of pants belonging to my ——. When I went back for them and for some dresses (fortunately they were calico and so washed), I noticed a very peculiar and disgusting odor. I remarked, "You can never be healthy in such an atmosphere as this. Why don't you open your windows?" "They have been open." The room was in semi-darkness, and a child's cot was in the corner. I believe now the sick child was in that cot. I took my effects and departed. The next day. Mrs. G——, a kind neighbor from that house, said: "You get your sewing done there? I want some done; but little Jeff, who went to get some milk there, says he is sure that he saw a child ill with small-pox, and refused to take the milk." "Can it be possible!" It flashed upon me instantly that was really the peculiar disgusting odor of small-pox I had smelt. I said so. A doctor was sent to investigate, and it was found to be the case; and the criminal neglect of that family gave it to ten parties in that street—one of them my son. A brother of little Jeff took it also. My patient had started on business and reached Toronto, feeling very ill; went to a physician there, who told him there was a good deal of low fever about, and he had better lay up in some hospital there. He said, no, he would come home; but, just on arrival, wanted to go to an hospital—

beginning to fear it was small-pox. But as it was late, and he very much exhausted, I persuaded him to stay with us for one night, as he had had no food and could take none. I gave him some hot bitter ale (an old Englishman had told me it was a good thing to cause an eruption to come out). He slept the sleep of exhaustion that night, and the next morning he was covered with a rash. We had been such a healthy family. We knew no doctor in Montreal; knew none to whom to apply. So (and now the personal pronoun must be used very often if I am to obtain the desired result from these memories) that by helping any one unexpectedly placed in my position, unable to procure medical help, I was enabled to take care of and preserve the life and prevent disfigurement of a patient, and destroy all danger of infection.

I called to Mr. G——, a neighbor, from an upper window, and asked him to send me a doctor. "What for?" "I don't know." "Can it be small-pox?" "It may be." So he sent. Dr. Laberge arrived, glanced from a distance, said "I'll send the doctor of the Civic hospital tomorrow. We'll judge better then." There was chloride of lime on a saucer in the passage, through which passed a through draft of air. There was no one in the house except my husband, my son and myself. My servant had gone home some days previously. My dear husband would not leave; but I never spoke to him, except from a distance, for six long weeks. He occupied a room in the lower story, and spent his days walking in the country, and took his meals out. The next day the civic doctor arrived— he pronounced it an unmistakable case of smallpox. "Will you have him taken to the Civic hospital?" was the next query? "Can I hire a room to go with him, and nurse him, if I stay inside all the time?" "No; there is no room to hire. The hospital is crowded. It will be as much as I can do to get your son a bed; then he will remain." The two next houses were unoccupied—parties were in the country. Mine was on a corner, next a large vacant lot, opposite a large green field, with an empty school-house. I decided to ask permission to remain. I again sent for Dr. Laberge; he took in the surroundings, and said I could, as he saw I was to be trusted. I asked him to attend my patient; he said he could not, in his public situation he would risk too much infection to others. "Well, then," I asked, "can you tell me how to make the salve Dr. Lafleur, of Levis (now deceased), put on the patient's face to prevent disfigurement? Was it black?" "No, grey." "This I cannot tell you; but I know in England they use something with charcoal in it." And that was all the medical advice I had in the course of this long and very serious illness, for it was a very bad case, and the doctor who had seen my son in Toronto said, from the weakness of my patient at the time he saw him, he thought that there were no hopes of recovery. I also sent for Dr. P———, of Bleury street. He looked in from the door, and said his duty to patients he was then attending would prevent his coming, unless in case of inflammation of the lungs or other serious complication. So I prepared for a seige in earnest. I talked from an upper window, and ordered that essence of beef and a bag of ship (not cabin) biscuits, be sent to me. Some canned things for myself, cheese, other crackers, honey, preserved fruit, lemons, oranges, gelatine and wine for jelly, etc.; and as medical stores an ounce of flour of sulphur, a bottle of iodine (small one), a jar of mineral water, a few ounces best cream of tartar, a small quantity of powdered charcoal, a box of pure fresh lard, a small new paint brush, a bottle of sweet oil, and a few seidlitz powders.

This was all my medical paraphernalia, more preventive than curative, for I pretend to no medical knowledge.

OTHER PREPARATIONS.

In the outbuildings was a table, with drawers, containing silver money over a cup of chloride of lime, paper, and pen and ink.

I arranged with a man to place on that table every day, a pound of any kind of fresh meat, some boxes of strawberries, half a gallon of milk, a few fresh eggs, and the daily papers. My friends were requested after ringing the bell to look to the parlor window, from whence I said how we were getting on, and to place between the doors amusing books, papers and letters. Well, with profuse apologies came the men. "So sorry, but we are obliged to placard you." "So much obliged," said I. "Put it on the outer door where it can be well seen, and then I shall have perfect quiet and not be bothered by visitors."

Now I think it is time to go back to my patient, whom I have left quietly dosing in the very top story on the bath room flat. For the first few days he was very weak, his long travel and anxiety to reach home had told upon him, so occasionally I gave him hot ale as nutritive and stimulating, and sailors' biscuits and strawberries. He was delighted with the biscuit. "How did you come to think of it. I could not have eaten bread." I know by experience that a person ill can eat sailors or soda biscuit when they cannot eat anything else; besides, the baker ceased to come, and if the man I had hired to bring me provisions failed me, I was insured against starvation, for none of my family would have been permitted to come near me. I have since learned, that when a house is placarded, you can insist on a policeman calling with eatables every day. As soon as the eruption was fully out, I made a salve of charcoal, perfectly black, with which the patient's face was thickly covered, he only looked like a negro, and as the oldest of everything was brought into use and burnt in a small stove on the same flat, it did not matter much. Old shirts shared the same fate, and for pocket handkerchiefs I used old squares of cotton, and burned them. Then I put into practice what Dr. LaFleur taught me. It sounds disgusting, but is not everything about small-pox disgusting, and a few days patience and perseverance protects from disfigurement for life. So I must tell you that *every single pustule as soon as it reaches maturity, must be picked with a clean fine needle,* and not suffered to eat holes in the skin, for this is what causes disfigurement, by small-pox. Then mix equal parts of cream and iodine, and with a small clean paint brush touch every pustule, don't neglect one, or there will be a mark. This must be done every day for a few days; if it smarts put more cream, and then every day for about a week, put on all over the face a mixture of cream and glycerine. That is the whole process, very simple in practice, and which not only saves the looks, but gives great relief, by taking away the intolerable itching which small-pox patients suffer from; for sore throat and inability to swallow, gargle with flour of sulphur, and put a little on the tongue. Now for diet. As soon as the eruption was fully out, I gave all fruit and milk he asked. I stopped the ale, and never gave a drop of wine or stimulant of any kind during the whole six weeks he was in my charge. I may state here that from what I have heard, I attribute the great disfigurement amongst the French Canadians, particularly of the lower class (intelligent people know better), to the great quantity of whiskey and gin given at that time. In fact, I heard a man say in the cars one day, there is only one remedy for small-pox, this about a young child—*du gin à force*—meaning gin in any quantity, and now mind ask a doctor what diet should be, as I had no doctor. I gave my patient what he asked for, tea, coffee, broma, lemonade, and when the fever was high lemonade with plenty of cream of tartar, for which this receipt :—

Take an ounce of cream of tartar, put it in a good sized jug, cut up a lemon and put it on the cream of tartar with some white sugar, pour on it some boiling water to extract the juice, then fill up with cold water, and when well settled, give as the patient is thirsty.

After the anxiety of the first ten days was over, and my patient began to mend, we had some very pleasant though quiet days. I read aloud amusing books and papers, and at the end of about six weeks I thought my patient well enough to go free, and so called out of the window to send for a city doctor to pronounce my patient cured. We went into the hangard, where a nice dinner was cooling on a coal oil stove, passed the day there while the house was being disinfected, and returned next day to freedom, with grateful hearts to rejoice over past danger. If I have been so minute in these details, it is that in times of public calamity, when doctors are overworked and hard to procure, most parties lose their wits, and do not exercise the calm judgment that might otherwise help to save their friends and themselves.

I must note as a singular fact that both the gentlemen I have spoken of as patients had been vaccinated as children, which shows the necessity of revaccination, while I, who attended them, had not been revaccinated, and, after a lapse of fifty years vaccination, never took it, though I attended them both. An extraordinary exception, not to be relied upon. The question was asked me, what would you have done if your patients became delirious, as you were alone? They were both at times slightly delirious, but not annoyingly so. Had they shown the slightest symptom of becoming uncontrollable, I should have rolled them in sheets, tied them, and called for help. I had reasoned out all my plans in my own mind. So I give this as a hint to others, and I advise any one else to bathe the feet constantly in sweet oil, as one patient suffered most from his feet. In cases of yellow fever, I have heard that in the South they apply a salt herring to the sole of the foot, it draws out the fever, becomes black, is burnt, and another put on. I would now try the same on small-pox, taking care the brine did not touch the skin, the herring to be well covered.

CHOLERA.

The first case of cholera I remember of was the case of a servant who was pronounced by two doctors almost in the state of collapse. A man—I never knew his name—asked to be allowed to try what he could do, as there was pronounced no hope. He tried brandy in good green tea, after a dose of castor oil,—I think a tea-spoonful of best brandy in a small cup of hot green tea. The women recovered, and, like wildfire, the news spread, and old Mr. Tibbits, recently deceased, and Horatio Patton, Esq., both lumber merchants, employing hundreds of hands, used to start out in the morning, on their rounds, each carrying a bottle of brandy and pail of hot tea in hands, waiting on and saving the lives of hundreds of men, women and children.

The late Brian O'Hara, Esq., a very old friend of my dear father's, told me that when a merchant in Porto Rico (he was English consul there), so many of his blacks died of cholera, that he was obliged to have a large dining room in his house prepared as an hospital, and the ladies of his family to look after them. Cold water was supposed at that time, in nearly all diseases, especially cholera, to be so much poison, and the men were, some of them, strapped down to prevent their getting at it. One powerful fellow, on seeing the men place water on the verandah, broke his bonds, and before he could be stopped, drank more than a quart; all expected to see him die, instead, he began to mend from that moment, and then the others were allowed to use it. None died after.

I had a very young child ill with country cholera. My father advised my trying cold water and giving the child ice to suck. My boy is living now. And a young doctor, living near us at Lake St. Charles, refused to try it, thinking it too hazardous a remedy. His child died. Water poured on chopped raw beef, allowed to soak to extract strength, is also good in cholera for a young child.

Now, cholera is much better understood; then its treatment was guess work. A physician, now deceased, who had a great deal to do with it (late Dr. Michaud, of Kamouraska), told me, from the first moment of an attack, if possible, one attacked should remain perfectly quiescent. The movement of a hand even being unwise.

PREVENTION.

Mrs. MacDonald, wife of a sergeant in the army (one of Quebec's noted nurses), told me that on the outbreak of the cholera in India, the doctor of the regiment ordered that every man, woman and child put on and keep on a flannel band, reaching from the waist to the hips, and not one of their regiment died of it. *Apropos* of cholera, the late Dr. James Sewell told me that when in England, staying with two old lady friends, one became ill. He said he had seen so much of it in Quebec he knew it was cholera by the peculiar look in the eye, and advised them to send for their own doctor at once. The learned man came and, after examining the lady, said it was nothing serious, and wanted to see this young prodigy from America who knew so much. The lady was dead before night of Asiatic cholera. The London physician knew it in theory, Dr. Sewell by practice. But even Dr. Sewell's well tried knowledge failed to save his cherished wife, who died of it after a few hours illness. The first symptoms must be attended to at once ; whereas this lady, seeing her husband so overworked, failed to acquaint him how ill she felt, and fell a victim in part to her own unselfishness. How great was the universal sorrow I need not say.

CANCER.

The late Dr. Anderson told me he had seen his father, I think it was, cure a woman by the application of pure lemon-juice. He said the lemon-juice killed the cancer, the bad flesh fell off, and the woman's shoulder remained perfectly cured without aid of the knife.

SPRAINS.

An Indian remedy for sprains is to take salted parsley and bind it on the sprained part, changing it occasionally till it is cured. This I know to be perfectly successful, having seen a party treated. Hot camomile infusive is also good for a sprain.

INDIAN REMEDY FOR DROPSY.

I was told that a woman who had lived near us some years ago, a farmer's wife, had been cured by a squaw, by covering the whole body with slices of cucumber which drew out the water through the pores, I do not know whether this is true or not, but it was told to me for a fact.

For sting of a wasp or bee, wet earth, and put it on, it will take away the pain at once.

To my Subscribers.

A word of thanks. Nearly all personal friends of half a century standing I have desired that a record may be kept of your names, a pleasing remembrance of the past. At the time I penned these old memories I had no idea of publishing them ; having done so I thank you, and on the success I achieve will depend whether or not I ever come before you again.

Charlotte Macpherson.

MONTREAL.

E. Arnoldi.
W. S. Taylor, treasurer C.P.R.
W. F. Suckling, assistant treasurer C.P.R.
S. E. Taprell, cashier C.P.R.
Dr. Kirkpatrick, Montreal General Hospital.
W. Grant Stewart, M. D.
G. W. Swett, Windsor Hotel, 2 copies.
J. Penfold, Bank B.N.A.
M. Michaels, Windsor Hotel, 2 copies.
E Macauley, Insurance.
J. W. McCallum, advocate.
Joseph Ringfield, 54 Victoria Street.
Mrs. E. Urquhart, do
Mr. R. Hall, do
Andrew Baille.
E. B. Meyer (Morgans).
J. C. Johnston, Courville Street.
Miss Duggan, do.
J. H. Michaud, 73 Mackay.
Lewis J. Trotter.
F. Meredith, Esq., barrister.

Chas. Austin, 11 Hospital Street.
H. Lindsay, Art Gallery.
Mrs. Kingston, Dorchester Street.
H. Girard, C.P.R.
Dr. LaBerge.
Provincial Board of Health.
Dr. Lachapelle, Board of Health.
G. A. Bowen, 53 Victoria Street.
W. D. Dawson, St. Lawrence Street.
Rev. G. Osborne Troop, 577 Sherbrooke.
Miss F. D. Joseph, 19 Milton Street.
Miss M. Milne.
R. G. Kelly, 21 Laval av.
E. B. Greenshields, 2 copies.
A. B. Chaffee, C.P.R.
Jno. W. Molson.
Dr. McKechnie, Montreal General Hospital.
Walter Paul.
W. D. Dupont.
Rev. Ed. Wood, St John the Evangelist Church.
A. Joyce, Cathcart Street.
W. Denoon, Peel Street.
J. H. Bouchette, 1 Drummond Street.
L. Barbeau.
Chs. Holland.
Ernest Stuart.
J. P. P. Casgrain.
J. Cradock Simpson.
Chs. Alexander.
Wm. Sharpley.
Theo. Robinson.
Geo. McKay, 1871 Notre Dame Street.
J. Alex. Strathy, 73 St. Frs. Xavier Street.
A. Bishop Stewart.
W. F. Smardon.
D. Walker, 2347 St. Catherine Street.
R. T. Takahashi, 2367 St. Catherine Street.
Saml. S. Grant. 72 Beaver Hall
Geo. E. Drummond

Strachan Bethune.
J. F. Gibsone.
Henry McKay, 233 Commissioners Street.
W. J. Anderson, 199 Commissioners Street
Jas. G. Shaw, 37 Shuter Street.
Mrs. F. A. Fuhrer.
C. Meredith, 87 St. Frs. Xavier Street.
A. Macnider, Bank of Montreal.
J. H. Pipon, Bank of Montreal.
U. Garand, Banque Ville Marie.
J. A. MacPhail, Mansfield Street.
Somerville Weir.
John Palmer.
C. F. J. Phillips, 1755 Notre Dame Street.
H. C. Scott.
L. J. R. Hubert.
M. Authier.
David Denne.
Gerald E. Hart.
David R. McCord.
Wm. McLennan.
Henry Fry.
W. Drysdale.
Forbes Torrance.
Miss Coleman, 54 Victoria.
Dr. Fenwick.
Alfred Monk, 180 St. James.

QUEBEC.

St. Louis Hotel.
W. G. Lemesurier.
Hon. Thos. McGreevy.
Hon. Pierre Garneau.
Lady Stuart.
Madame J. T. Taschereau.
Hon. M. Stearns, Legislative Assembly.
Archibald Campbell, Esq., Prothonotary.
John Burroughs, Esq., Prothonotary.
Louis Fiset, Esq., Prothonotary.
C. P. Angers, Lieut-Gov.

The Ursuline Convent.
J. J. Foote, Chronicle.
Mercury office.
George Van Felsan.
E. Chinic.
Hon. David Ross.
Ernest Hamel.
H. Hope Sewell.
Henry Austin, notary.
M. Cook, advocate.
J. D. Dawson.
Robert Mitchell.
H. W. Wright.
James Carrell, Telegraph Co.
St. Leon Mineral Water Co., 5 copies.
J. H. Philips, St. Leon Water Co.
Rev. J. H. Petry.
C. E. Holiwell, bookseller.
Auger & Campbell, notaries.
Arthur Hunt.
Daniel McGee.
Jas. A. Macnider.
J. Stevenson, Quebec Bank.
E. G. Meredith, notary.
H. M. G. McMichael, manager Bank B. N. A.
J. C. Moore, Merchants B. of Canada.
P. G. LaFrance, Banque Nationale.
P. B. Dumoulin, Banque du Peuple.
Matthew Miller.
W. Lindsay Creighton, Bank of Montreal.
A. Thompson, president Union Bank.
E. G. Price, vice-president Union Bank.
E. J. Hale, director Union Bank.
D. C. Thompson, Union Bank.
E. E. Webb, cashier Union Bank.
D. Rickaby.
Behan Brothers.

TORONTO.

Arthur Lobb.

www.ingramcontent.com/pod-product-compliance
Lightning Source LLC
Chambersburg PA
CBHW020118170426
43199CB00009B/563